STEP-BY-STEP

BARGELLO

By Geraldine Cosentino

Evans Brothers Limited London

This case-bound edition first published in Great Britain 1975
by Evans Brothers Limited, Montague House, Russell Square, London WC1B 5BX
First British edition published 1975 by Pan Books Ltd.

© Western Publishing Co. Inc. 1974

ISBN 0 237 44833 5

Acknowledgments

I wish to thank Susan Rudin for designing and making up the tie and the child's footstool, and for her work on many of the patterns and projects in the book. I would also like to thank Christine Swirnoff for designing and making the carrier bag, the table runner and napkin rings, the pincushion, and the Bargello rug. Many thanks also to Binnie Weissleder for allowing me to use her drawing as the basis of the pineapple picture, to Phyllis Safer of the Brooklyn Public Library for help in obtaining material, and to Caroline Greenberg who edited this book.

Geraldine Cosentino

Art Director: Remo Cosentino
Art Assistant: Diane Wagner
Editor: Caroline Greenberg
Illustrations: Liz Green
Photographs: George Ancona

Printed in England by Cripplegate Printing Co. Ltd., London and Edenbridge.

Contents

NOTE ON METRICATION

Canvases are numbered according to the number of threads to the inch. At the time of going to press it had not been decided whether this system would continue after metrication; canvas will be sold by the metre and measured according to the number of stitches to the centimetre, but in spite of this the old numbering may remain the same.

At present the length of needles is measured in millimetres and the gauge in imperial; again, at the time of going to press it had not been decided whether they would be numbered according to the Continental system or whether the same method would be continued.

Rug wool is available in weights of 10, 20, 25, 40 and 50 grams and in multiples of 50.

An eighteenth-century Italian wall hanging combining a needlepoint border with Bargello work in the centre. (Photo courtesy of The Metropolitan Museum of Art, Gift of Mrs Samuel Stiefel, 1938.)

Introduction

Bargello, also called flame stitch or Florentine stitch, is an old form of canvas embroidery similar to needlepoint. Many interesting, if untrue, stories exist about its origin. The name Bargello comes from a museum in Florence, where there is a set of chairs dating from the seventeenth century that were embroidered in a type of Bargello called Hungarian Point. The Bargello Museum was at one time a prison, and one story has it that a Hungarian noblewoman spent her time there teaching the prisoners embroidery.

The same Hungarian lady was supposed to have married a Medici and brought Hungarian Point to Italy as a decoration on her trousseau. The origin of this style of work is said to have occurred at a time when there was a great shortage of wool, and Hungarian Point was supposedly invented in order to use most of the wool needed in the design on the front of the work and as little as possible on the back. An examination of any piece of Hungarian Point will bear this out.

The origin of the Florentine stitch is uncertain, but it undoubtedly derived from the brick stitch, a vertical needlepoint stitch that resembles tiny rows of bricks in a wall. This brick stitch is found in many early pieces of European embroidery, often used as a background for other motifs.

Medieval craftsmen, who worked with a limited colour range of natural dyes, relied on shading to give variety to their work. This is the origin of the many shaded patterns that we see in Bargello even today. Another early Bargello pattern still used is the carnation, which dates back to Elizabethan England. Bargello embroidery was used in Italy, England, Spain, and Colonial America, where examples of it can be seen in the restored village of Williamsburg, Virginia.

Bargello was used for the upholstery of chairs, curtains, bed valances, and rugs. Small objects were also made of Bargello: pincushions, tops for needlework boxes, wallets and purses. Early samples included Florentine stitch and Hungarian Point patterns.

The art of canvas embroidery declined in the nineteenth and early twentieth centuries. After World War II, embroidery re-emerged as a creative art along with other crafts, such as weaving, rugmaking, candlemaking, knitting and crocheting. Today, other old forms of embroidery like crewelwork and needlepoint as well as Bargello have become increasingly popular, whereas only a few years ago even their names were unfamiliar.

A man's Early American wallet or purse done in a carnation pattern, with the name of the owner embroidered on it. (Photo courtesy of the Museum of the City of New York.)

Bargello is a form of vertical needlepoint in which the patterns are formed by the length and placement of the stitches on a canvas backing. By counting the threads or meshes of the canvas vertically and horizontally, all kinds of forms can be created: peaks and valleys, curves, diamonds, flames, bars, stripes, latticework. These patterns cover the canvas more quickly than needlepoint because they are always worked over at least two and sometimes as many as eight threads of the canvas at once. This makes Bargello fast and easy to do. Since Bargello stitches are made vertically, there is little need for complicated blocking because the canvas is never pulled out of shape. Bargello work offers more creativity than is found in the traditional needlepoint designs already printed on the canvas because of the variety of stitches and patterns that are possible. There are few things more relaxing to do than needlework, and the finished pieces, pictures or cushions add a great deal of warmth and charm to our homes.

In the following chapters we will be discussing the different stitches and patterns used in Bargello embroidery and their practical uses. We will also explain the different materials that are needed to create them, and help you to understand a little more about colour.

This book contains a variety of projects both decorative and practical, some easy to make, some difficult. Sewing and finishing instructions are also included so that projects can be made from start to finish at home.

This Queen Anne-type wing chair from 1725 is worked in Florentine stitch in a variation of the carnation pattern. (Photo courtesy of The Metropolitan Museum of Art, Gift of Mrs J. Insley Blair, 1950.)

Materials

The basic materials for Bargello work are canvas, yarn and needles. You will want some additional equipment and other optional accessories to make your Bargello embroidery pleasant and easy to do.

CANVAS

Canvas is the foundation of your Bargello piece. It is essentially a loosely woven mesh or net. The number of threads or meshes to the centimetre (inch) indicates the size of the canvas. The fewer stitches there are, the more open the weave. Canvas can be so fine that it resembles woven gauze or it may be as coarse as only one or two threads to the centimetre.

The type of piece you wish to make will indicate the number of the canvas you need. A rug or cushion done in heavy yarn would use a very open canvas such as a No 4 or No 5, but a small, delicate, or intricate piece or pattern would call for a much finer canvas. Most Bargello patterns are done on canvas having five, six or seven meshes to the centimetre.

There are two distinct types of canvas. One has a double thread or mesh consisting of two threads woven very closely vertically and two threads woven more loosely horizontally. This is known as penelope or double mesh canvas. The other type is a single mesh called mono canvas. Penelope or double mesh canvas often comes in ecru and mono canvas in white.

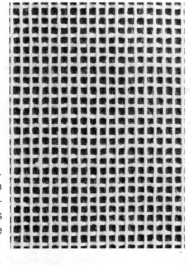 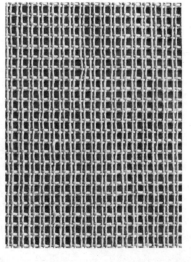

(Right) Mono canvas, No 10 mesh. (Far right) Penelope or double mesh canvas, No 10 mesh. Notice the difference between the double woven threads in penelope canvas and the single threads in mono canvas.

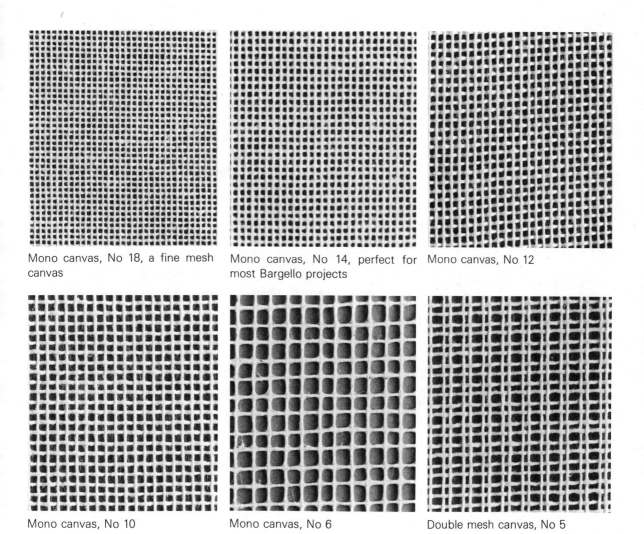

Mono canvas, No 18, a fine mesh canvas

Mono canvas, No 14, perfect for most Bargello projects

Mono canvas, No 12

Mono canvas, No 10

Mono canvas, No 6

Double mesh canvas, No 5

Canvas is sold by the metre and comes in different widths ranging from 60 to 90 cm. Be sure that you know the working dimensions of your project before you buy so that you will get the correct width of the canvas. Always look for an even weave and a highly polished canvas. Do not accept any canvas that appears to be knotted or woven irregularly. This indicates poor quality and may spoil your work.

If at all possible, check the size of the mesh before you buy. Mislabelling *can* occur, and you may ask for No 12 canvas and find when you are home that you have No 14 instead. The selvedge of the canvas is usually worked on the side of the piece, not the top or bottom, so be sure to take this into consideration when calculating the amount of canvas you must buy.

YARN AND THREAD

Yarn and thread come in many varieties, but usually one type is more suitable than others for a particular kind of work. The thickness of the yarn must be in proportion to the size of the canvas mesh you are using so that the backing will be fully covered and not show through. Fine yarns can be doubled for use on a coarse canvas; thick yarns can sometimes be separated for use on a fine canvas. Generally, the lower the number of meshes to the canvas, the thicker your yarn must be; finer yarns or threads should be used on canvas with a higher mesh number.

Persian wool. Persian wool is a three-strand twisted yarn of lustrous wool and comes in a great variety of colours. It is the most brilliant and long-lasting of the yarns and also the most expensive. It is ideal for use on No 10 or No 12 canvas when doubled and is used on No 14 canvas single. The strands can be separated for finer work on finer canvas or for mixing to form a new shade.

Tapestry wool. Tapestry wool comes in four unseparable strands and a large colour range. You can double tapestry wool to create a thicker texture. Tapestry wool is excellent for most Bargello projects. It is used singly on No 12 or doubled on No 10 mono canvas.

Crewel wool. Crewel wool is a fine wool strand available in many colours. It is usually for for embroidering on fabric, but it can be used successfully on very fine mesh canvas.

Rug yarn. Rug yarn is a very heavy three-ply yarn that is ideally suited to No. 5 canvas. It comes in a variety of colours and in a rayon-cotton mixture as well as wool.

Knitting yarn. Knitting yarns are not the best choice for Bargello embroidery. This type of wool tends to stretch more than tapestry or Persian yarn and is not as long-wearing. Its advantages are an enormous range of colours and textures and its relative cheapness in price. Sometimes an angora or other fluffy thread when combined with tapestry or Persian yarn can create an interesting textural effect without sacrificing the long-wearing quality of the other yarns.

Embroidery or pearl cotton. Cotton embroidery threads can replace wool for certain projects. Cotton has the advantage of being extremely long-wearing, and comes in a great variety of colours with either a mat or pearl finish. It is impervious to moths and can be washed or dry-cleaned with good results. It is important to select the right canvas so that the cotton will cover it completely.

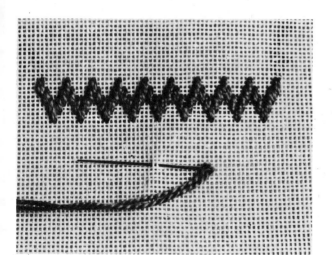

Cotton embroidery yarn on No 18 canvas, doubled

Crewel yarn on No 14 canvas

Persian yarn on No 14 canvas

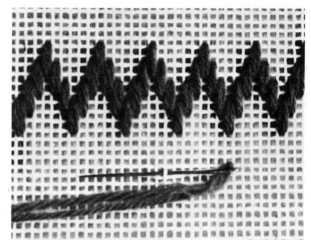

Tapestry yarn on No 10 canvas, doubled

Knitting yarn on No. 10 canvas, doubled

Rug yarn on No 5 double mesh canvas

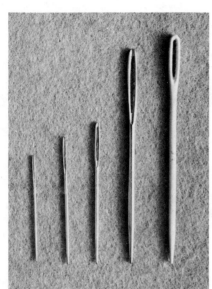

Different needle sizes, from left to right: No 24, 20, 18, 13, and a plastic needle for heavy wool

NEEDLES

Needles used for Bargello embroidery are called tapestry needles and have a blunt end with a large eye. They come in a variety of sizes from No 13, which is used on a No 5 canvas for rugs and quickpoint, to No 24, a very fine needle used on the finest canvas. The best needles for most Bargello embroidery are Nos 17 to 20, with a No 18 a good all-purpose choice. When not in use, store your needles in a small container. While sewing, frequently run them through an emery bag needle sharpener to keep them clean.

ADDITIONAL EQUIPMENT

A storage basket or large container for all your yarns, canvas and other equipment is a good idea. You can keep your work there when not in use, and store all your yarns in one place. If you get into the habit of keeping everything in one spot, it prevents you from mislaying your work—and ensures that everything will be at hand when you need it.

Scissors are another very useful item. You will need heavy shears to cut your canvas and to handle large quantities of wool to be cut into convenient strands for working. You will also need fine scissors for cutting the excess yarn on the back of the work, and for ripping out that occasional wrong stitch.

Masking tape is necessary to bind the edges of the canvas before you begin. This prevents the canvas from fraying and tearing, and also prevents the wool from catching on the rough edges and breaking.

A steel ruler is also useful. It can be used for marking and measuring the dimensions of your work, for measuring the canvas before you cut, and for ruling lines.

Felt-tip marking pens in several colours are good for marking lines on the canvas, provided they are indelible. They can be used to indicate the centre of the work or for indicating the finished dimensions. Felt-tip markers can also be used for sketching designs and working out colour schemes.

A notebook is nice for jotting down ideas on future projects or to indicate where you are in the project at hand. It can be useful as a written reminder of things to be done.

If you are interested in plotting your own designs, graph paper is an essential. You can accurately chart your own designs or copy others. Graph paper comes in different sizes and rulings, often with measurements indicated. It is a wise idea to work with large graph paper at first, and then, when you are accustomed to it, to try to obtain paper as close to the size of the canvas as possible.

Heavy carpet thread and darning needles can be used to tack down the raw edges of your work — either before it is finished, or as part of the finishing process. If you sew with a thimble you may want to use one for Bargello. If so, make sure that it fits comfortably, neither too tight nor too loose.

One of the pleasures of most needlework is its portability; it is truly handwork in the sense that you can carry it in the hand as well as work it by hand. In Bargello an embroidery frame is not necessary. It may even stretch some work out of shape if not used properly.

Some of the supplies needed in Bargello work: a basket for wools, scissors, ruler, thread, pincushion with emery bag needle sharpener, graph paper, notebook, felt-tip markers, tape, wool and canvas

Stitches

The basic stitch used in Bargello embroidery is always a vertical one. It may cover anywhere from two to eight meshes of the canvas, but it must always do so in a straight line. Certain stitch lengths and combinations occur frequently and have come to have specific names, such as Florentine stitch and Hungarian stitch.

Other types of stitches combine well with Bargello stitches and are used in conjunction with them, either as background or border stitches. There are also stitches, known as finishing stitches, that are used to finish or bind off work. Once you become familiar with this repertoire of stitches you will find that they add a great deal of variety and enjoyment to your work.

FLORENTINE STITCH

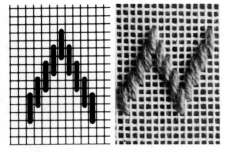

Florentine stitch

This is the most often used stitch in Bargello embroidery as it is found in a number of patterns and designs such as flame, zigzag, diamonds, and curves and points (see pages 15-19). This stitch is made by inserting the needle into the canvas and covering four meshes vertically up, and then re-inserting the needle and bringing it out for the next stitch two meshes down in the next vertical line. This stitch is known as the four-two stitch: that is, four steps up and then two down. This forms a staggered vertical line going upward. To go down you simply reverse the procedure and go down four and then back up two. This stitch is generally worked throughout an entire pattern. Florentine stitch can also mean any vertical stitch whose steps are in the ratio of two to one: for example, 2:1, 4:2, 6:3, 8:4 and so on.

HUNGARIAN STITCH

Hungarian stitch

The Hungarian stitch is composed of one short stitch, one long stitch, and then one short stitch. A space is left and then the procedure is repeated: one short stitch, one long stitch, one short stitch, space. The short stitch covers two meshes of the canvas while the long one usually covers four and is centred between the two short ones. Each row of long stitches fits into the preceding row's skipped space. That is how the long points which are formed are fitted into the pattern. Hungarian stitch is a good filler when you want a textured background area.

BRICK STITCH

The brick stitch resembles its name, as it consists of rows of upright stitches all the same length but spaced to resemble the alternating pattern of rows of tiny bricks. The brick stitch can be made in two different ways. One method is to work horizontally, leaving a space between each stitch, and then come back and fill in either one mesh above or below to form the pattern. The other method is also worked horizontally, but in this case the stitches are alternated: one up, one down, one up, one down. Following rows are then fitted in to continue the pattern.

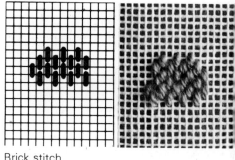

Brick stitch

GOBELIN STITCH

The Gobelin stitch is named after the type of stitch used in the famous French Gobelin tapestries. This stitch usually covers two to four meshes of the canvas vertically and is used in horizontal rows only. When it is used in combination with other Bargello stitches, care must be taken to see that each horizontal row is uniform with the others throughout the piece.

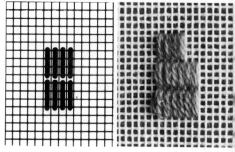

Gobelin stitch

SATIN STITCH

The satin stitch is found in most types of embroidery. It is made by covering the same number of meshes in one horizontal or diagonal area. This stitch gives rather a padded look to your work, as the back and front are equally covered. This can result in a bumpy piece of work if the rest of the stitches do not cover the back and front of your canvas in a similar way.

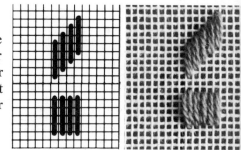

Satin stitch (bottom), oblique satin stitch (top)

DIAMOND STITCH

As its name indicates, the diamond stitch forms diamond shapes. It is made by increasing the length of each stitch until the longest stitch is reached and then decreasing again in exactly the same ratio. For example, the first stitch will cover two meshes; the next, four, one above and one below the preceding stitch; the next stitch, six; and then the longest, eight. Decreasing now, the next stitch will be six, corresponding to the six before the eight; the next, four; and the last, two. Any number of stitches can be used depending on how large you wish to make the diamond.

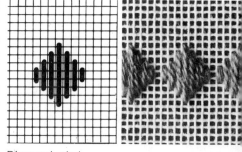

Diamond stitch

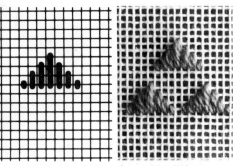

Half-diamond or pyramid stitch

HALF-DIAMOND OR PYRAMID STITCH

This stitch is used as a border stitch and forms pyramids, or half-diamonds. It is made like the diamond stitch except that the bottom of each pyramid is straight, and the top of the stitch increases by only one mesh. For example, the first stitch will cover one mesh; the next stitch, two; the next, three; and the longest stitch will cover four meshes of the canvas. The stitches then grow progressively shorter. Three, two, and finally one mesh are covered and you have completed the pyramid.

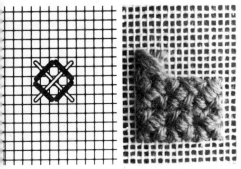

Rice or crossed corners stitch

RICE OR CROSSED CORNERS STITCH

Another border stitch is the rice stitch, also called the crossed corners stitch. This stitch should be used sparingly, as it can pull the canvas out of shape because it is basically a diagonal stitch. The rice stitch is really a large cross-stitch with tiny crosses made over each of the corners. A cross-stitch is made, each arm of the cross covering four meshes of the canvas. Then a tiny diagonal stitch is made over each corner of the cross, two going to the right and two going to the left. You may find it necessary to divide the thread in half for these tiny stitches so that they will not appear too bulky.

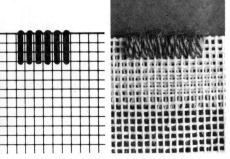

Whip stitch over edge of canvas

WHIP STITCH

One of the best and easiest ways of finishing off a piece of work is with the whip stitch. This stitch is particularly useful on smaller projects such as spectacles cases, chokers and bookmarks. The margins of the piece must be folded into place and tacked down with carpet thread, allowing the edge of the canvas to be left bare. The whip stitch will fill up the last empty row (or rows) and form a finishing edge over the top of the canvas. The yarn is passed through the canvas from the back to the front and over the top to the back again. It is basically the same as the whip stitch in sewing.

Patterns

Bargello patterns can be divided into two groups: those in which the stitches are all the same length, and those in which the stitch length varies. These patterns are called Florentine stitch and Hungarian Point respectively. Florentine stitch may occasionally include one or more short stitches in the pattern, but this is done for purposes of accommodation. The overall effect should be one of a continuous line of stitches of the same size. Hungarian Point is characterized by variation in stitch length, usually two or three short stitches to every long one. Most of the patterns that follow will be in Florentine stitch, as this offers the greatest variety in pattern and motif.

Bargello patterns are essentially repeat designs. Once the shape or line has been established it always reappears in a regular sequence. A change in canvas size or yarn colour can change the appearance of a pattern radically. A pattern on a small-mesh canvas using only a few colours will seem to reappear constantly, but the same pattern on a large-mesh canvas using many colours may never seem to repeat itself.

When selecting a pattern you must ask yourself certain questions. Do you want something small and unobtrusive, something that will add to or blend in with a particular colour scheme; or do you want a dynamic accent piece that will stand out because of its bold colours and large design? Once you have decided what your particular needs are, study the portfolio of patterns that follows. These are among the most often seen and used Bargello patterns. Some of them are hundreds of years old and some are extremely modern. All can be used in a great variety of projects.

Note: The patterns on the following pages were made on mono canvas with fourteen meshes to the inch. Single strand Persian yarn was used throughout.

The scallops pattern shown below was done on two different sizes of canvas. The sample on the left was done with Persian yarn on No 14 canvas. The one on the right was done with rug yarn on No 5 canvas.

Zigzag pattern

Flame pattern

Scallops pattern

Byzantine domes pattern

Diamond pattern

Deep boxes pattern

ZIGZAG

The zigzag pattern is the simplest and most basic Bargello pattern. It is a line pattern, which means that once the basic line has been established it is continued row after row in exactly the same way throughout. The zigzag is shown here in three contrasting colours. It can be done this way or in shaded colours. The stitch is the Florentine stitch, and it is done with the same number of stitches ascending as descending.

FLAME

The flame pattern is similar to the zigzag because it is also a line pattern, and it, too, uses the Florentine stitch. The difference is that the line is uneven, with the ascending and descending points of unequal length. This uneven line and the colours, which range from yellow through reds to brown, give it its name. If this same pattern were done in ice white to blue, it could be called ice crystals.

SCALLOPS

The curved effect in the scallops pattern is created by repeating a stitch before going on to the next one: one, two, three, five, three, two, one. It is filled in in the same way, decreasing the number of stitches needed to fill in the shapes. This is an overlapping motif. One scallop fits into the next one, giving a three-dimensional effect. Florentine stitch was used except for two tiny stitches on one of the lines to maintain the pattern. Four colours — yellow, orange, red, and maroon — were used to create a light to dark effect.

BYZANTINE DOMES

This pattern is an enclosed motif with a common outline. The exaggerated curves occur because of the repetition of the stitch before moving up or down. This pattern looks best when done in contrasting rather than shaded colours. The stitch covers four meshes of the canvas throughout.

DIAMONDS

One of the most popular patterns in Bargello is the diamond. It can be used vertically or horizontally, as it is perfectly suited to the stepped quality of the Florentine stitch.

DEEP BOXES

This design is strongly three-dimensional. Five shades of one colour form the boxes. Black is used to fill in and give a deep dimensional effect. All stitches are done in pairs and cover four meshes of the canvas. This pattern can be considered a variation of the diamond shape.

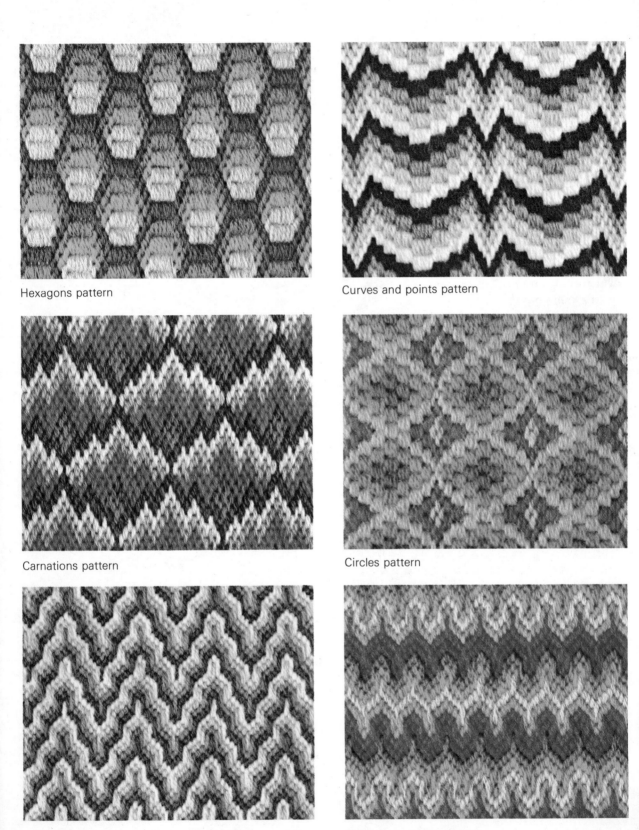

Hexagons pattern

Curves and points pattern

Carnations pattern

Circles pattern

Hungarian point pattern

Hungarian stripes pattern

HEXAGONS

The hexagon pattern is an extremely modern-looking one because of its geometric shape. It is considered an enclosed pattern because it is not a continuous line throughout but a motif which is enclosed in a dark outline. This pattern was done in Florentine stitch in three shades of turquoise, with a dark blue outline. The hexagon pattern should always be done in shaded colours going from light to dark.

CURVES AND POINTS

This is a linear pattern done in Florentine stitch over four threads of the canvas. It is worked in white, black, and two shades of grey, but it can be done in other colour combinations. This is an old pattern and can be used most effectively for larger items where the pattern can be seen to advantage. The curves are created by repeating a stitch a number of times before going either up or down.

CARNATIONS

Variations of the carnation pattern date back to Elizabethan England. This pattern was also popular in Colonial America. The flower is worked in shades of rose while the stem and outline are done in green. All stitches cover four meshes.

CIRCLES

This is an old pattern of circles with diamond shapes formed in the interstices. It can be used for a large area piece, or one strip of the circles can be used for a narrow border or edging. All stitches cover four meshes of the canvas.

HUNGARIAN POINT

The Hungarian Point pattern is a linear one. Once the initial line has been established it repeats once every three lines. This happens because the stitch length is irregular: two short stitches covering two meshes of the canvas to one long one covering five. The pattern can be worked in shaded colours as shown or in contrasting tones.

HUNGARIAN STRIPES

This pattern is done in a variation of the Hungarian Point pattern. The long stitch here covers six meshes and the short one covers three. It is done in six colours: yellow, orange, red and three shades of turquoise. The design is intricate because of the variety of the repeat. The lines repeat once every four horizontal rows, but the colours repeat only once every six rows. This means the pattern does not repeat itself until twelve lines have been completed. It is ideal for small items.

Colour

The beauty of Bargello lies in its subtle use of colour and pattern. Depending on the colours used, a piece can look quiet and restful or bold and exciting. Colour creates its own atmosphere because of its emotional and psychological associations. For example, certain colours give us definite feelings. Red and yellow look cheerful and exciting, while blue and green look peaceful and calm.

A basic colour vocabulary will help to explain certain technical terms which will be used later in the chapter.

Hue – the actual colour something is – for example, red, blue.

Value – whether a colour is light or dark.

Intensity – how bright or dull a colour is.

Tint – a colour that has been mixed with white.

Shade – a colour that has been mixed with black. This term is also used generally to mean any value, light or dark, of a particular colour – for example, a shade of blue.

Tone – a colour that has been mixed with both black and white to make it look greyer.

Complementary colours – two colours that become grey when mixed together optically.

Primary colours – red, blue, yellow.

Secondary colours – colours mixed from the primaries: orange, violet, turquoise, green, yellow-green.

Cool colours – blue, green, violet; colours that recede.

Warm colours – red, yellow, orange; colours that advance.

Achromatic colours – these are not really colours at all because they have no hue, just value: black, white, grey.

Monochromatic colours – all the values from light to dark that exist in one colour.

THE COLOUR WHEEL

An important tool in creating colour schemes that look attractive is the colour wheel. This is a circle of colours in a specific arrangement where each colour has a particular relationship to all the others. A simple colour wheel would be arranged in this way: yellow, orange, red, violet, blue, turquoise, green, yellow-green. This wheel (facing page) contains three primary colours and five secondary colours. The secondary colours are made up as follows: orange from yellow and red; violet from red and blue; green from yellow and blue; turquoise from blue and green; and yellow-green from yellow and green.

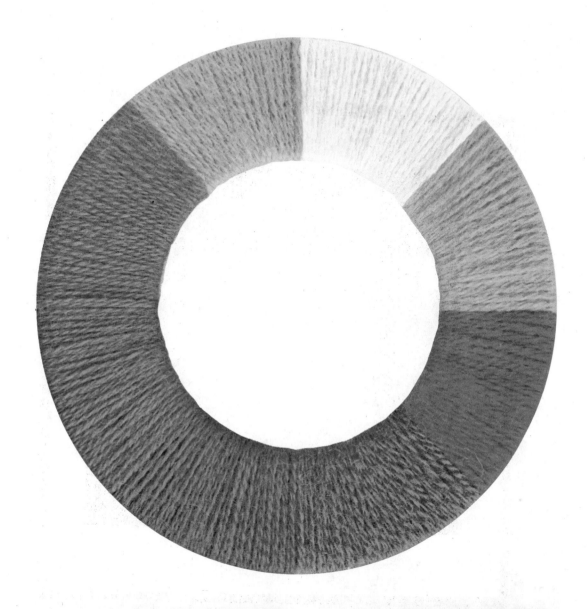

(Above) Five shades of one colour, going from light to dark. (Right) Matching colours to a pattern diagram.

A four-way Bargello picture done in concentric squares

For a harmonious colour scheme, with colours that will always look well together, select two or three colours that are next to each other on the colour wheel. If you wish, you can add to this basic scheme by using the shades and tints of these colours as well, thus creating a wide range of tones without a confusing effect.

Avoid using any two colours which are opposite each other on the colour wheel. They are complementary colours and will .create a negative grey feeling; they will cancel each other's effectiveness no matter how bright they are.

SHADING

To create the shaded effect that is so popular in Bargello embroidery today, you must use a monochromatic colour scheme based on the use of one colour and all its tones. To choose colours for this kind of project it is best to see them in daylight. Take individual strands of the colours you have chosen and hold them next to one another in the order in which they will be used in the design. Try to have the same step, or difference in value, between each colour. Bright and light colours tend to look slightly darker when they are worked. Some of the subtle greys and lavenders that are found in the old, shaded Bargello patterns result from garish colours having faded to lovely muted tones quite different from the original ones.

To get a three-dimensional effect, it is necessary to work with colour intensities. Bold, bright colours in your design will appear to come forward while the greyer, blacker ones will seem to recede even though they are all on the same level.

COLOUR IDEAS

When trying to decide on which colours to use for a Bargello project, there are some useful pointers to keep in mind. Always limit the number of colours used. Too many different colours produce a confused effect. A variety of shades of one or two colours provides contrast and avoids flatness. Try to have one light, one or two medium, and one dark colour in your scheme.

The character of a colour is changed by the colours surrounding it. Orange, for example, will stand out among cool colours but will blend with warm ones. A black background intensifies colours, especially light ones. White will set off darker colours.

Bright colours are a good choice for upholstery patterns, such as those for chair seats or footstools, because they will allow for some fading (no matter what claims manufacturers make, yarns *do* fade with time).

And most important of all — remember that the use of colour is an individual preference. Your eye should be the final judge.

Sewing and Finishing

Although it is hard to imagine, Bargello embroidery can last 200 years. With the proper tools and techniques, your projects should last for an indefinite time without showing signs of wear. In order to avoid costly mistakes and to create technically sound work at home, the following methods will be useful.

BEFORE YOU BEGIN

Choose your pattern and project with care. For instance, Hungarian Point, because of its irregular backing, is not recommended for chair seats and other items which will receive a lot of wear. Have a clear idea in mind of the purpose of the finished work, whether it is to be practical or to be decorative, and select your materials accordingly.

Make sure that you have the proper relationship of yarn or thread to canvas and needle. Too thin a thread produces flecks of canvas showing through the work and will not wear well. (If necessary, you can double your thread to cover the canvas properly.) Select a needle with the proper eye for the yarns and canvas you are using.

Estimating yarn quantity. You will want to be sure to buy enough yarn for your project. Dye lots vary, and you may not be able to get a good match if you run out of yarn. Do not be afraid to overestimate; leftover yarns can always be used for small items.

To estimate the amount of yarn you will need, work a 5-cm (or 2-in) square of your pattern and measure the length of each of the yarns you are using. Divide this number by 25 (or 4 if you are measuring in inches) and then multiply by the total number of square centimetres (or inches) in your canvas and you will arrive at an approximation of the length you will need. Most suppliers will be glad to help you estimate the amount of yarn necessary for a project if you are able to tell them the size of the finished piece, the pattern and the number of colours you are using.

PREPARING THE CANVAS

To prepare the canvas for working, you must cut it to the right size. Allow a generous margin of at least 2.5–5 cm (1 or 2 in) around the finished dimensions of the piece. Then tape the edges of the canvas with masking tape to prevent them from fraying and the yarn from catching on the raw edges. To do this you must cut a piece of 2.5-cm (1-in) wide masking tape slightly longer than the length of one side of the canvas. Place it so that half the masking tape is under the canvas edge and half is free. Press the edge of the canvas down so that it adheres to the tape.

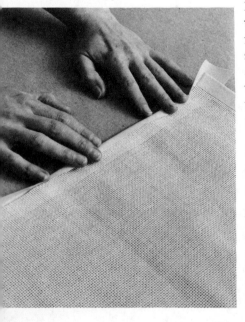

Taping the canvas. Fold tape over the edge of the canvas so that it adheres to both sides.

Then fold the free edge of the tape over to the other side of the canvas as if it were binding tape. Press this edge down with your fingers and the canvas edge is covered. Repeat this procedure until all edges of the canvas are covered. If you wish, you can also run a row of machine stitching around the edges.

You are now ready to place the design on canvas. If you use a marker to indicate the margins of your piece, make sure that it is waterproof by testing a small spot on the canvas. Wash it with soap and water or steam it with an iron to see if it will run. Bargello designs should be done by counting canvas threads, so do not mark the canvas too much or rely on measuring with a ruler. The canvas meshes can vary over a number of centimetres, and this can be enough to throw your design off. If you are following a graph-paper chart, each square on the chart will equal one mesh on the canvas. Count the squares to find the number of meshes to be worked.

CENTRING THE PATTERN

If you are using a repeat motif, rather than a line pattern, centre the motif on your canvas and work all the others in relation to that one so that the design will be even on all sides. To centre a design, you must find the centre of the canvas and work the design from that point out. To find the centre, fold the canvas in half vertically and then in half horizontally. The centre of the canvas is where the two folds meet. Place a pin or make a mark there to use as a guide.

(Below left) Folding the canvas in quarters to find the centre. (Below right) Marking the centre after the canvas has been folded.

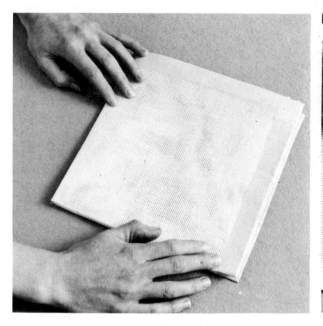

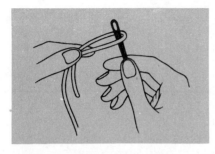

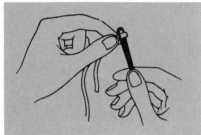

Another method of threading a needle is to loop the yarn over the needle and then press it tightly around the needle. Remove needle, leaving a flat loop. Press eye of needle over the folded yarn and pull through.

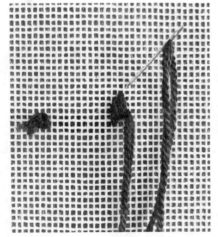

Start your work with a knot on the right side of the canvas about an inch away from the first stitch.

SEWING TECHNIQUES

Before you start to sew you must thread the needle correctly. Do not lick the yarn; just press a folded strand between your finger and thumb until the yarn is flat. Then press the eye of the needle over the folded yarn and the needle is threaded. Thread several needles with yarn so that you do not have to stop and thread needles continuously. Do not work with yarn that is longer than 45 or 60 cm (18 or 25 in), especially knitting yarn. This length is easiest to work with and does not knot or twist as readily as longer pieces. Yarn starts to fray or stretch after being pulled through the canvas too many times.

It makes no difference if you are right- or left-handed when starting to work. After starting at the centre, it is possible to work in any direction you find comfortable: left to right, right to left, top to bottom. Each person will develop the individual working method that is most suitable for him.

Do not knot the thread; this creates lumps in the finished work. (Too many thread ends in one spot will also create a bumpy look.) Instead, allow about 2.5 cm (1 in) of yarn to remain on the wrong side. Anchor it with your thumb or a finger while you work the first stitches so that it will remain secure. An alternative beginning method is to place a knot on the right side of the work about 2.5 cm (1 in) away from where you want to begin. After you have worked a number of stitches, cut the knot and pull the excess thread to the back.

With a linear design, once you establish the first — or tracking — line all you have to do for the rest of the pattern is to follow that line. **With an enclosed motif,** it is easier to do all the outline stitches first. After that, just fill in.

To end off the yarn, do not knot it. Slip the needle through a few stitches in the back of the work and then cut the thread. To start a new thread, run your needle through a few stitches on the back of the canvas and come up at the proper spot.

Work with the yarn at an even tension, not too tight. If the yarn becomes twisted, hold the canvas upside down and the needle will fall free and unwind itself. If you are working on a large canvas, roll up the part you are not using.

Make sure that all points in the pattern line up correctly. If a stitch does not fit into the pattern, it means there is a mistake somewhere that will have to be ripped out. To rip it out, carefully cut the wrong stitch on the front with embroidery scissors and pull out the loose threads with a tweezer. Never reinsert the needle to take out stitches. The yarn can become badly entangled and you can split existing stitches or even some threads of the canvas. Never reuse old yarn.

If you accidentally cut the canvas, repair it by placing a small patch of canvas cut just a little larger than the rip. Tack the patch on and sew through the two thicknesses.

Remember to run your needles through an emery bag from time to time to keep them clean and sharp.

To check for missed stitches, hold the finished work up to a strong light and any missed stitches will show up as blank spots.

FINISHING TECHNIQUES

The best piece of work can be ruined if good finishing techniques are not followed. As much care must be taken when finishing a piece as when embroidering it. In general, hand-finishing is best.

Bargello needs very little blocking. A light pressing on the wrong side with a steam iron will refresh and resquare it. It is a good idea after blocking to machine-stitch a row of stitching around the worked portion of the canvas as close as possible to the yarn to prevent loosening or unravelling of the embroidery. This can be done by hand in a back stitch. Do not cut the margins from the canvas until any blocking or cleaning has been done and you are ready to finish it, because a rectangular piece of canvas will keep its shape longest.

Onto the back of every finished piece of needlework weave two or three strands of every colour you have used. You will then have matching yarn for any needed repair work later on. Spray finished pieces with Scotchgard fabric protector. (If the work becomes dirty, it can be dry-cleaned. Take it to a reputable cleaner and tell him the fibre content of the yarn and canvas.)

When you are ready to finish your work, cut off all but a 1- to 2.5-cm (½- to 1-in) margin all around for sewing. It is a good idea to mitre the corners before folding back the edges and sewing them to the back of the canvas. Cut a small square out of each corner of the canvas, leaving only one or two meshes of unworked canvas. Dab some white glue on each of the corners and let it dry. This prevents the canvas from ravelling. Now fold back all the unworked canvas and sew it to the back with heavy thread. This technique is used when you are making anything requiring a backing or lining to be sewn onto the finished embroidery.

Machine-finishing. A heavy-duty needle and heavy-duty thread must be used when sewing by machine. Pin or tack all pieces together to prevent shifting while sewing. It is necessary to sew into the wool a little when sewing by machine, so if you are using this method, allow a margin of embroidery for this purpose on your finished work.

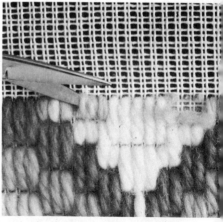

Rip out stitches carefully by cutting them on the front of the work.

A child's footstool. This is a patchwork Bargello design, done in brightly coloured Persian wools.

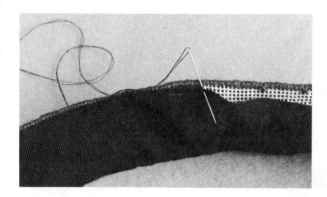

LININGS

Linings and backings for Bargello pieces should be tightly woven. Felt is a good choice, as it is sturdy, comes in many colours, and does not have to be hemmed. Polyester double-knit fabric is excellent for linings because it does not ravel, and iron-on fabrics are handy because they do not require sewing. Grosgrain ribbon is a good backing for belts and other small items. Always buy the ribbon the same width as the piece you are backing. When lining spectacle cases, protect the lenses by using a soft fabric. Iron-on interfacing, obtainable from drapers', provides a convenient way to give body or stiffening to Bargello projects. It also prevents items from being pulled out of shape. If you want to give a soft look to a piece of needlework, insert a layer of foam rubber or layered dacron between the backing or lining and the canvas.

CUSHIONS

To back cushions, choose fabrics in a colour and texture that will complement the design you have used. Velveteen, corduroy and cotton suede make excellent backings. Knife-edge cushions are the easiest to make; they are usually edged with a welting or fringe, or finished with tassels (see page 34).

To make a knife-edge cushion form: Cut two pieces of muslin or old sheeting the size needed, seam on three sides, turn inside out, stuff with foam rubber or cotton, and sew closed.

Boxed cushions are a bit harder, but if you would like to try one, follow the directions on page 38.

BELTS

Be sure to use what I have called 'self-closing' belt buckles for the projects in this book — they eliminate the need for punching holes in the needlework. It is a good idea to work a belt at least 5 cm (2 in) longer than the desired waist measurement — to allow for adjustments and for sewing on the buckles.

(Above left) Sewing the backing to a belt. (Above right) Assembling the finished Bargello work, cushion stuffing, and backing fabric to finish a small pincushion.

Projects

Waves cushion

Finished size: 27 x 28 cm (10½ x 11 in)

Materials

Three-ply Persian yarn – dark violet 42 gr (1½ oz), medium violet 28 gr (1 oz), light violet 28 gr (1 oz), very light violet 28 gr (1 oz)

Mono canvas, 4 meshes to the centimetre (10 meshes to the inch), 38 x 38 cm (15 x 15 in)

No 18 tapestry needle

Velvet backing material; thread to match

Cushion form

Masking tape, scissors, marker, ruler, needles

Stitches: Florentine over 4 meshes, Gobelin over 4 meshes. Yarn doubled in needle throughout.

This cushion is very simple to make because it is a linear pattern. Once you have established the initial line, all you do is continue the succeeding rows in exactly the same way until the desired size is reached.

Directions: After you have assembled your materials, the first step is to cut the canvas. Measure carefully and cut the canvas to 38 x 38 cm (15 x 15 in). This will allow a good margin all round. Remember that the selvedge should be at the side of your work. Bind all four edges with masking tape. Find the centre of the canvas by folding it in half vertically, and then horizontally. The centre is where the folds meet. Mark it with a cross.

Next, measure the working size of your canvas. This will be 13.5 cm (5¼ in) above the centre and 13.5 cm (5¼ in) below the centre. Measure and mark these top and bottom margins with a line. Measure 14 cm (5½ in) horizontally from the centre on either side to find the side margins. Mark each with a line also. You should now have a marked area of 27 x 28 cm (10½ x 11 in), the finished size of your cushion. Before starting work it might be helpful to review the section on sewing and finishing (page 24)

The stitch used in this pattern is the Florentine over 4 meshes of the canvas, with a step up or down over 2 meshes, and the Gobelin over 4 meshes of the canvas. The pattern is formed in this way: four Florentine stitches up, four horizontal Gobelin stitches, four Florentine stitches down, four horizontal Gobelin stitches. These sixteen stitches are repeated to create the line. The colour order is as follows: dark violet, medium violet, light violet, very light violet; and then very light violet, light violet, medium violet, dark violet. These eight colour rows are repeated, always starting and ending with the darkest shade. If

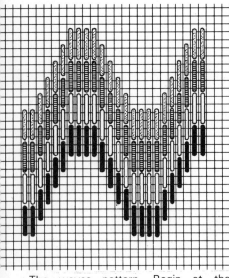

The waves pattern. Begin at the bottom left corner of the canvas and continue across.

Waves cushion

you wish to begin at the top or the bottom of the cushion, use the darkest colour. If you start at the centre, use the lightest.

The entire horizontal line covers 112 meshes. Follow the pattern diagram on the facing page for the correct placement of the stitches. Do this line twenty-four times to complete three colour repeats. Fill in the unworked top and bottom areas with dark blue to create the effect of a background.

Finishing: Trim the excess canvas to approximately 2.5 cm (1 in) all around. It is best to finish the cushion by hand since the thickness of the needlework makes it difficult to use a sewing machine. If necessary, block the needlework by ironing it lightly on the wrong side with a damp cloth.

Cut the backing fabric to approximately the same size as the canvas, including the 2.5-cm (1-in) seam allowance. Place the right sides of the needlework and the fabric together and sew around three sides, including the four corners, with a back-stitch seam. Turn the cushion right side out and insert a cushion form (to make your own, see page 29). Blind-stitch the fourth side closed.

Vertical stripes cushion. The attached tassels add a decorative touch.

Vertical stripes cushion

Finished size: 36 x 36 cm (14 x 14 in)

Materials

Rug yarn, rayon and cotton – one 110-gr (4-oz) skein each of beige, rust, orange

Double mesh canvas, 2 meshes to the centimetre (5 meshes to the inch), 45 x 45 cm (18 x 18 in)

No 13 tapestry needle

Backing material; thread to match

Cushion form

Masking tape, scissors, marker, ruler, needles

Cardboard and yarn for tassels (optional)

Stitch: Florentine over 2 meshes. Yarn doubled in needle throughout.

The vertical stripes cushion is done on large-mesh canvas with rug yarn. Even though the stripes are vertical instead of horizontal, this pattern can be considered linear. Care must be taken when making the stripes, because only the beige stripe is continuous – the rust and orange stripes intertwine. This cushion can be worked vertically from top to bottom or *vice versa* as you prefer.

Directions: Cut the canvas to 45 x 45 cm (18 x 18 in) and bind all edges with masking tape. Indicate the actual working area 5 cm (2 in) in from each edge on all sides. Mark the margins, especially the corners, so you know where to start.

Find the bottom left-hand corner of your work area. Using the beige yarn, take a stitch over 1 mesh of the canvas at the corner and come out 1 mesh to the right, but still at the bottom margin. This is a half stitch. Take another stitch over 2 meshes of the canvas and come out one mesh up and one over. Continue until you have one half stitch and ten whole stitches. Change direction and go to the left, making another ten whole stitches. Continue vertically, changing direction every ten stitches until you reach the top margin. Finish with another half stitch.

Make a second line of beige next to the one you have just completed. Then skip 8 meshes horizontally and begin another beige stripe. (The 8 skipped meshes will be used for the rust and orange stripes.) Continue until you have made six double lines of beige stripes.

Now you are ready to start the rust stripe. Begin exactly as you did with the beige, by taking one half stitch over the first mesh and then continuing with nine whole stitches. Start at the bottom again and do another line of eight whole rust stitches and one half rust stitch.

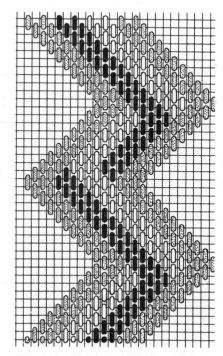

The vertical stripes pattern. Start at the bottom left-hand corner of the canvas and work vertically, not horizontally.

Three steps in making a tassel. Wind the yarn around the cardboard, secure, and cut. Bind the top. Trim the yarn ends and attach the finished tassel to the cushion.

Thread your needle with orange and start at the bottom next to the rust stripe. Start with a half stitch in orange and then do eight whole stitches. Do not stop here: simply change direction and continue with twelve more orange stitches. Start again at the bottom edge and repeat the orange line.

Now thread your needle with rust again and start eight stitches up; do a row of fourteen vertical rust stitches, change direction, and do seven more. Go back and do another row of rust stitches next to the one you have just finished.

Continue alternating the rust and orange stripes until you have reached the top margin of the cushion. Do four more rust and orange stripes. You should now have six beige stripes and five rust and orange stripes. Fill in the side margins with the angles of the rust and orange stripes to complete both sides.

Finishing: Trim the excess canvas from the completed needlework, leaving a 2.5-cm (1-in) margin on all sides. Cut a piece of backing material the same size as the trimmed canvas, including the 2.5-cm (1-in) seam allowance. Place the right sides together and seam by hand on three sides and four corners. Insert a cushion form (to make your own, see page 29) and carefully sew the fourth side closed.

Tassels add a decorative touch to this cushion. To make them, wind yarn around a piece of cardboard cut about 25 cm (10 in) long. The more times you wind the yarn, the thicker the tassel will be. Slip a length of yarn under the wound yarn at one end of the cardboard and tie. Cut through the yarn at the opposite end of the cardboard. Cut another length of yarn and wrap it 2.5 or 5 cm (1 or 2 in) below the tie for the head of the tassel. Make four and fasten one to each corner of the cushion.

Red, white and blue sampler cushion

Finished size: 34 x 39 cm (13¼ x 15½ in)

Materials

Tapestry wool – red 42 gr (1½ oz), white 42 gr (1½ oz),
    blue 56.5 gr (2 oz)

Mono canvas, 4 meshes to the centimetre (10 meshes to the inch),
    45.5 x 51 cm (18 x 20 in)

No 18 tapestry needle

Velvet backing material; thread to match

Boxed cushion form

Masking tape, scissors, marker, ruler, needles

Stitches: Florentine over 2 meshes, Florentine over 4 meshes, Hungarian point variation, rice, pyramid. Yarn doubled in needle throughout (except in the rice stitch, as indicated below).

This cushion (pictured on page 37) is made from four different patterns and two border stitches. It is not advised for the beginner. The four different patterns are curves, interlocking diamonds, intersecting diamonds, and Hungarian waves. The border uses the rice stitch and two varieties of the pyramid stitch.

Directions: Cut a piece of canvas approximately 45.5 x 51 cm (18 x 20 in) and bind all four sides with masking tape. Next, and most important, divide the canvas into four equal areas. Do this by folding the canvas in half vertically and drawing a line down the length, and then folding the canvas in half horizontally and drawing another line across the width. Since each pattern is based on a 60-mesh count, count 60 meshes from the centre line horizontally on either side and mark your side margins. Then count 60 meshes up and 60 meshes down from the centre and mark your top and bottom margins. You should now have four equal areas, each one 60 meshes long and 60 meshes wide. Number them 1, 2, 3, and 4 in clockwise order. These numbers correspond to the patterns described below.

The first pattern to start is No 1, curves. This is the easiest pattern in the cushion since it is linear, and once the first line is completed the rest are exactly the same. The line consists of three curves, each one covering 20 meshes of the canvas. The colour order is red, white, blue, red, white, blue. The stitch is Florentine over 2 meshes of the canvas and the yarn is doubled. Start at the bottom of square No 1 and make one complete line in blue. Continue up, using the appropriate colours, until you have finished the square. Finish the pattern by filling in the appropriate portions at the top and bottom margins.

Pattern No 2 is called interlocking diamonds. There is no common line; each diamond fits into the one above and below it. The outlines alternate red and blue, with a white inner diamond and a contrasting centre.

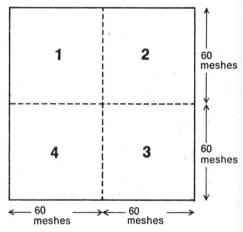

Divide and number the canvas for the four different pillow patterns as shown above.

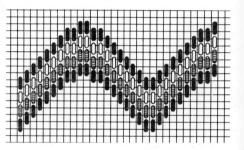

Pattern No 1, curves. Start at the bottom left of pattern area No 1.

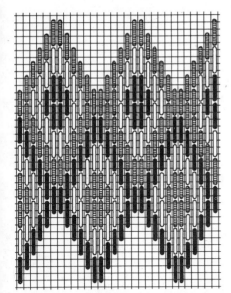

Pattern No 2, interlocking diamonds. Start at the centre left of pattern area No 2.

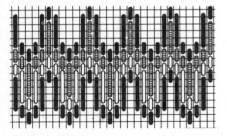

Pattern No 3, Hungarian waves. Start at the centre left of pattern area No 3.

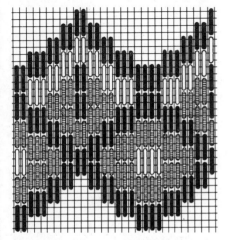

Pattern No 4, intersecting diamonds. Start at the centre left of pattern area No 4.

The stitch is Florentine over 4 meshes of the canvas and the yarn is doubled. Start by counting 28 meshes up from the bottom of square No 2. Thread your needle with red wool.

Using the Florentine stitch, make the upper half of the red diamond five times. You should now be at the right margin of your work area. Turn the canvas and complete the bottom halves. Fill in the centres before going on to the outline of the blue diamonds. Start either right above or right below the red diamonds and make four whole and two half diamonds in blue. Fill in the centres. Complete the pattern area by filling in a little more than half of the red diamonds.

Pattern No 3, Hungarian waves, uses a variation of the Hungarian Point pattern, with its characteristic short, long stitch pattern. In this design we have two short stitches, each one over 2 meshes of the canvas, to one long stitch over 5 meshes. The red line follows this pattern while the blue and white lines vary in order to accommodate the long stitch. The colour pattern is red, blue, white, each colour line having a different stitch pattern. The yarn is doubled.

Count up 30 meshes and start with the blue line. Continue in the appropriate sequence until you come to the margins. Fill in the entire square to finish the pattern.

Pattern No 4, intersecting diamonds, consists of two differently shaped diamonds that share a common outline but have different centres. There are three rows of three whole diamonds with a filling consisting of a white top, a blue centre, and a red bottom, alternating with two rows of whole diamonds and half diamonds having a flower-like red filling with a white centre. The stitch used is Florentine over 4 meshes with the yarn doubled. Since this is the most difficult pattern of the four, follow the accompanying diagram carefully for the correct placement of the colours and stitches. Start at the left margin, 30 meshes up, to form the centre row of three complete diamonds. Finish the blue outlines first and then fill in the centres.

After all four patterns have been completed, work a border in blue around the entire cushion with the rice stitch. With the yarn doubled, work over a 4-mesh square for the initial crosses; use yarn single in needle for the crossed corners. (See page 14 for exact instructions for making this stitch.) Next, with yarn doubled, work a border of pyramid stitches in white covering 1 to 4 meshes of the canvas. Then fill in the remaining spaces with a row of blue pyramid stitches covering from 1 to 3 meshes of the canvas. As each corner is worked, adjust it individually to fit.

Red, white and blue sampler cushion, backed and boxed in blue velvet. (Right) A detail of the cushion centre showing the four pattern areas.

Detail of red, white and blue sampler cushion showing the border stitches.

Finishing: Trim the finished canvas to 2.5-cm (1-in) margins on all sides. If necessary, block the needlework by ironing on the wrong side with a damp cloth. Turn the 2.5-cm (1-in) margins to the back of the needlework and slip-stitch in place.

For a boxed cushion, cut two strips of velvet backing fabric 12.5 cm (5 in) wide by 75 cm (29½ in) long. Stitch one end of each of these strips together with 1.25-cm (½-in) seams to form boxing strip. For the back, cut a piece of velvet the same size as the finished needlework plus a 1.25-cm (½-in) seam allowance all round. With right sides together, stitch one edge of the boxing strip to the back piece. Slip-stitch the needlework to the other side of the boxing strip, leaving one end open. Insert a cushion form and close the opening.

Climbing stairs trinket box

Finished size: 11 x 17.8 cm (4½ x 7 in)

Materials

Three-ply Persian yarn – 28 gr (1 oz) each of lavender, violet, dark purple

Double mesh canvas, 4 meshes to the centimetre (10 meshes to the inch), 19 x 25.5 cm (7½ x 10 in)

No 18 tapestry needle

Trinket box

Iron-on fabric for backing

Glue

Masking tape, scissors, ruler, marker

Stitches: Gobelin over 5 meshes, diamond and half-diamond over 1 to 5 meshes. Yarn doubled in needle throughout.

The optical illusion of climbing stairs is created by the different stitches, and by using a light, medium and dark shade of one colour. This kind of pattern looks best on a box with simple lines.

Directions: Select the trinket box you wish to use and carefully measure the top. In the case of the box illustrated, the top measured 11 x 17.8 cm (4½ x 7 in). Cut a piece of double mesh canvas at least 3.5 cm (1½ in) larger on each side than the box top. Tape all four sides with masking tape. Carefully mark the exact dimensions of the box top on the canvas. The pattern repeats every 15 meshes, so 11 cm (4½ in) represents 45 meshes, a multiple of 15, or three repeats of the pattern.

The Gobelin stitch was started in the lower left-hand corner margin over the first 5 meshes, and the pattern was worked out across the bottom row. Once the initial pattern line was started it was easy to follow for the remainder of the piece. If the size box you are using proves difficult to start in this way, centre the pattern instead. Find the centre of the canvas by folding it in half vertically, and then horizontally. The centre is where the folds meet. Mark it lightly with a cross and make the middle Gobelin stitch coincide with this centre mark. Work the pattern out on both sides from there and continue according to the diagram until you finish.

Finishing: Trim the canvas to a 2.5-cm (1-in) margin all around. Remove a small 4-mesh square from each of the corners to reduce the bulk when folding. Fold back the margins and fasten them to the back of the work. Cut a piece of iron-on fabric the exact size of the finished needlework. Following manufacturer's directions, iron it to the back of the finished work. Position the needlework on the box top and glue it in place with either white glue or an epoxy, depending on the material the box is made of. (Select glue according to label specifications.)

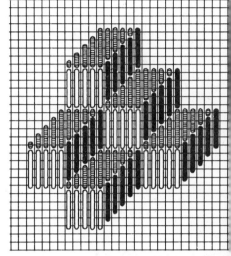

The climbing stairs pattern. Start with the Gobelin stitch in the lower left-hand corner or the centre of the canvas.

Climbing stairs trinket box.

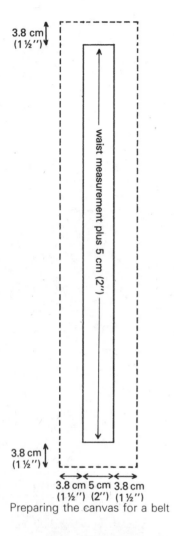

3.8 cm
(1½")

waist measurement plus 5 cm (2")

3.8 cm
(1½")

3.8 cm   5 cm   3.8 cm
(1½")   (2")   (1½")

Preparing the canvas for a belt

Rainbow belt

Finished size: 5 cm (2 in) wide; length as desired

Materials

Three-ply Persian wool – less than 14 gr (½ oz) each of red, orange, yellow, chartreuse, green, turquoise, violet, blue

Mono canvas, 5 meshes to the centimetre (12 meshes to the inch), 12.7 cm (5 in) wide x desired length plus 12.7 cm (5 in)

No 18 tapestry needle

Grosgrain ribbon, 5 cm (2 in) wide x length of belt; thread to match

Self-closing belt buckle

Masking tape, scissors, marker, tape measure, needles

Stitch: Florentine over 4 meshes. Yarn single in needle throughout.

Belts are among the easiest and most attractive items that can be made in Bargello. They are completed very quickly and make unusual presents. The pattern for this belt is a very simple chevron design covering 24 meshes of the canvas. The belt is pictured in colour on page 43.

Directions: Measure your waist and add 12.7 cm (5 in). Cut a strip of canvas 12.7 cm (5 in) wide and the length of this adjusted waist measurement. Tape the strip all around with masking tape. Mark off an area 24 meshes wide, about 3.8 cm (1½ in) in from the edges of your canvas. This corresponds to 5 cm (2 in), the width of the belt. Mark off the waist measurement plus 5 cm (2 in) for the length to be worked. Start at either end of the belt, following the diagram for the stitches. Make three rows vertically of each colour following this sequence: yellow, orange, red, violet, blue, turquoise, green, chartreuse and then yellow again.

Continue until you have reached the desired waist measurement. Fill in the areas remaining at either end with the correct colours.

Finishing: Trim the excess canvas to about 2.5 cm (1 in) on all sides, snipping out about one 1-cm (½-in) square of canvas at each corner to reduce the bulk when folding. Turn the edges under and tack them to the wrong side of the belt so that only the finished canvas is showing. Cut the grosgrain ribbon the length of the belt, allowing about 1 cm (½ in) at each end for a hem. Turn this raw edge under and sew the ribbon carefully to the canvas. Attach a belt buckle to each end of the belt, adjusting to the size of the waist measurement. (Be sure that you use a self-closing belt buckle, otherwise the belt will not be long enough.)

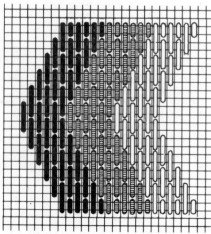

The rainbow pattern. Start at either end of the belt and work across.

Florentine circles belt

Finished size: 5 cm (2 in) wide; length as desired

Materials

Three-ply Persian yarn – beige 14 gr (½ oz), medium brown 28 gr
    (1 oz), dark brown 14 gr (½ oz), red 28 gr (1 oz)
Mono canvas, 6 meshes to the centimetre (14 meshes to the inch),
    12.7 cm (5 in) wide x desired length plus 12.7 cm (5 in)
No 18 tapestry needle
Grosgrain ribbon 5 cm (2 in) wide x length of belt; thread to match.
Self-closing belt buckle
Masking tape, tape measure, scissors, marker, needles

Stitches: Florentine over 4 meshes, Gobelin over 2 meshes.
Yarn single in needle throughout.

This belt (pictured on page 43) is adapted from an old
Florentine pattern of circles and diamonds. Only one row of
circles was used and a border stripe was added at either side.

Directions: Measure your waist and add 12.7 cm (5 in). Cut a
piece of canvas 12.7 cm (5 in) wide and the length of this
adjusted waist measurement. Tape all edges with masking tape.
Mark off an area 28 meshes wide, about 3.8 cm (1½ in) in from
the edges of the canvas. This corresponds to 5 cm (2 in), the
width of the belt. Mark off the waist measurement plus 5 cm
(2 in) for the length to be worked. Fold the canvas in half and
mark the centre back. This belt is worked from the centre back
to each front end so that it will be symmetrical on each side.

Thread a needle with dark brown wool. Count up 12 meshes
from the bottom margin at the centre back. Start the first circle
here. Follow the diagram for the circle pattern, leaving 2
unworked meshes at the top and bottom of the belt for the
border stitch. Make the circles first and then fill them in with
medium brown and red. Outline the area between the circles in
light beige and fill in with medium brown. Work the top and
bottom 2-mesh border in the Gobelin stitch in red. Complete
half the belt. Then do the other half the same way.

Finishing: Trim the unworked canvas to about 2.5 cm (1 in) all
around. Iron the belt on the wrong side if necessary to restore its
shape. Cut a 1-cm (½-in) square from each corner to reduce the
bulk when folding. Bend back the raw edges and tack them to
the wrong side of the belt so that no unworked canvas is
showing. Cut the grosgrain ribbon to the length of the belt plus
1.25 cm (½ in) on each end. Slip-stitch the ribbon to the belt,
turning under the excess at each end so that no raw edge of
ribbon shows. Attach the buckles to the ends of the belt, sewing
them securely into place, and fasten.

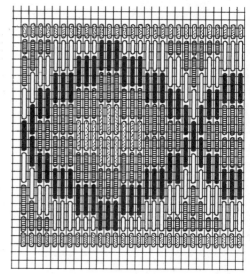

The Florentine circles pattern. Start
at the centre back of the belt and work
around to each end.

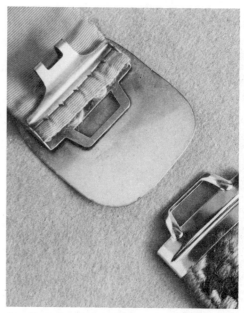

A self-closing belt buckle.

Zigzag belt

Finished size: 2.5 cm (1 in) wide; length as desired

Materials

Pearl cotton No 3 – one skein each of cream, pink, red; two skeins
  of blue

Mono canvas, 7 meshes to the centimetre (18 meshes to the inch),
  5 cm (2 in) wide x desired length plus 12.7 cm (5 in)

No 20 tapestry needle

Ribbon, 2.5 cm (1 in) wide x length of belt; thread to match

Self-closing belt buckle

Tape measure, scissors, marker, ruler, needles

Stitch: Varying stitch lengths, from 1 to 3 meshes; whip stitch border.
Yarn single in needle throughout.

The zigzag pattern of this belt is linear, and the long edges are
finished in the whip stitch.

Directions: Measure your waist and add 12.7 cm (5 in). Cut the
canvas 5 cm (2 in) wide by the length of this adjusted waist
measurement. Mark off the waist measurement plus 5 cm (2 in)
for the length to be worked. Then mark off an area 19 meshes
wide, about 1 cm (½ in) in from the edges of the canvas, for the
actual pattern of the belt, including the whip stitch border.
Bend back the excess at each long edge of the belt, giving you a
strip about 2.5 cm (1 in) wide. Tack excess canvas down in a
loose tacking stitch, making sure the meshes at the back of the
fold line up with the meshes at the front. Find the centre back of
the belt strip by folding it in half. Start the pattern here.

Begin with cream thread. Count up 10 meshes and start the
pattern at the high point of the line. Work the cream line until
you have finished half the belt. Next, do the pink line above and
below the cream. When necessary, sew through the doubled
mesh as if it were single canvas. Next, work the red line above
and below the pink, pulling out the tacking threads as you come
to them. Fill the remaining spaces with the little blue triangles,
making sure that you leave a 1-mesh margin throughout.
Complete half the belt this way, and then do the other half.
Finish the 1-mesh margin on both sides with the whip stitch over
the edge in blue.

Finishing: Trim the excess canvas at the two ends to about 2.5
cm (1 in); bend the excess pieces to the back of the work and
sew them down. Cut a piece of 2.5-cm (1-in) wide ribbon the
length of the belt, allowing an extra 1 cm (½ in) for hems. Sew
the ribbon carefully to the back of the belt, turning the raw
edges under at each end. Attach a buckle to each end of the belt,
adjusting to desired size. Sew securely in place, and fasten.

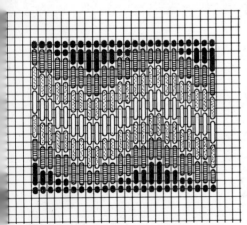

The zigzag pattern. Start at the centre
back of the belt and work around to
each end.

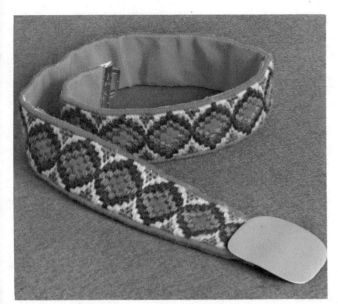

Florentine circles belt (instructions on page 41).

Zigzag belt (instructions on page 42).

Rainbow belt (instructions on page 40).

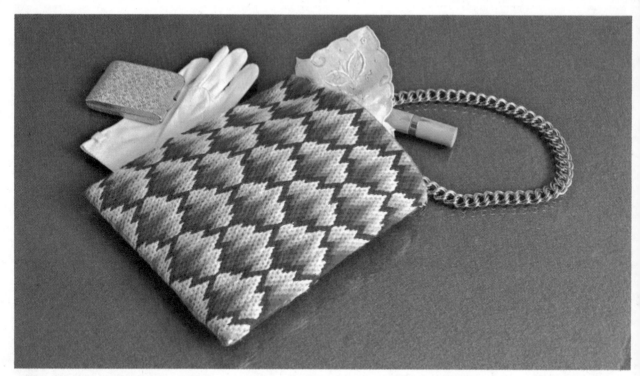

Carnation shoulder bag with a chain shoulder strap (instructions on page 45).

The double diamonds evening bag has an envelope flap closing and is lined with green felt (instructions on page 46).

Carnation shoulder bag

Finished size (before folding): 21.5 x 44.5 cm (8½ x 17½ in)

Materials

Three-ply Persian yarn – six shades of rose, 28 gr (1 oz) each
Mono canvas, 6 meshes to the centimetre (14 meshes to the inch),
    30.5 x 56 cm (12 x 22 in)
No 18 tapestry needle
Lining material; thread to match
Chain for shoulder
Masking tape, scissors, marker, ruler, needles

Stitch: Florentine over 4 meshes. Yarn single in needle throughout.

This bag is based on a very old Bargello pattern, and although each carnation fits one into the other, the top and bottom points do not line up.

Directions: Cut a piece of mono canvas 30.5 x 56 cm (12 x 22 in). Tape all raw edges. Measure an area approximately 21.5 x 44.5 cm (8½ x 17½ in) and lightly mark the margins. Fold the canvas in half horizontally and draw a line at this centre fold 21.5 cm (8½ in) long. This will be the point where the bag is folded. Following the pattern diagram, outline with the darkest colour four carnations, the width of the bag, with the bottom stitches falling on the centre fold line. Turn the canvas around and do the same thing on the other side. You should now have an area in the centre of the canvas which consists of the top halves of three whole and two half carnations. Since this pattern is not symmetrical, you must have one row of symmetrical shapes in the middle so the pattern will match at the sides when the bag is folded.

Continue outlining the carnations, reversing the pattern on the other side of the bag until you have outlined the entire working area. Now fill in the carnations with the remaining five colours, going from light to dark, with the lightest pink at the top of each carnation. When you fill in the centre row at the fold, use only the light colours for the carnation tops on either side.

Finishing: If necessary, iron the finished needlework on the wrong side with a damp cloth to restore the shape. Trim the canvas on all sides, allowing a 2.5-cm (1-in) margin. Fold this back and stitch it to the wrong side of the work. Cut a piece of lining material the size of the finished needlework plus a 1.25-cm (½-in) hem allowance. Turn the raw edges of the lining material under and stitch. Slip-stitch the lining to the canvas, wrong sides together. Fold the bag, matching the pattern exactly on both sides. Sew the sides together from the outside with stitches sewn between the Bargello stitches. They will sink into the wool and not be noticeable. Attach a shoulder chain.

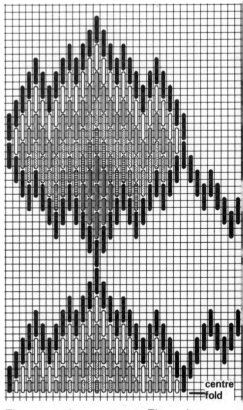

centre fold

The carnation pattern. The chart corresponds to the right-hand corner of the centre fold line for the bag. Be sure to reverse the pattern on the other side of the centre fold line.

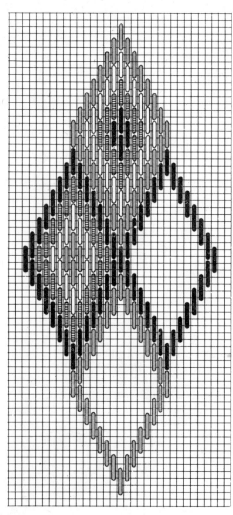

The double diamonds pattern. Begin at the centre of the canvas.

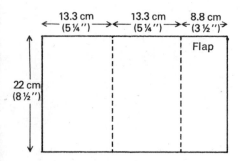

Fold the canvas along the lines shown to make the envelope and flap of the bag.

Double diamonds evening bag

Finished size (before folding): 21.5 x 35.5 cm (8½ x 14 in)

Materials

Three-ply Persian yarn – black 42.5 gr (1½ oz), dark blue 28 gr (1 oz), turquoise 42.5 gr (1½ oz), yellow-green 28 gr (1 oz)

Double mesh canvas, 4 meshes to the centimetre (10 meshes to the inch), 31.5 x 45.5 cm (12½ x 18 in)

No 18 tapestry needle

Felt lining material; thread to match

Snap fastener

Masking tape, scissors, marker, ruler, needles

Stitch: Florentine over 4 meshes. Yarn doubled in needle throughout.

An evening bag in Bargello is a lovely accessory that will last a lifetime. This one is pictured on page 44.

Directions: Cut the canvas to measure 31.5 x 45.5 cm (12½ x 18 in). Tape all sides. Find the centre of the canvas (see page 25) and mark off the area to be worked: 21.5 x 35.5 cm (8½ x 14 in). Thread a needle with black wool, doubled, and start at the centre mark by outlining the top halves of three black diamonds. Turn canvas around and complete the bottom halves. Then outline the other half of the row of black diamonds, making sure you have outlined six in all. Fill in each one as shown: dark blue, turquoise and yellow-green.

Next, begin the yellow-green diamond row. Find the centre of the canvas again. Insert the needle directly underneath the first stitch made in black. This stitch joins the third and fourth black diamonds. Begin to outline the tops of the yellow-green diamonds. When you reach the end of the row, stop. Count down 32 meshes from the top of the last yellow-green stitch, insert your needle, and begin to outline the bottom halves. The yellow-green diamond row is different from the black diamond row because there are two half and five whole diamonds instead of six. Fill in the yellow-green diamonds with colours in this order: turquoise, dark blue, black in the centre. Continue working one row of diamonds after another until you have completed the bottom half of the pattern. Finish by making a row of black half-diamonds. Turn your work around and finish the other side in the same way.

Finishing: Trim the excess canvas to 1.25 cm (½ in) all around. Fold this back and sew to the wrong side of the canvas. Cut a piece of felt the same size as the finished work and slip-stitch it to the canvas. Fold the bag according to the diagram and sew the side seams from the outside, matching the pattern and colours carefully. Sew a snap fastener under the flap to close the bag.

Peaks and waves bag

Finished size: 25.5 x 30.5 x 10 cm (10 x 12 x 4 in)

Materials

Three-ply Persian yarn—56 gr (2 oz) each of deep red, fuchsia,
  dark pink, medium pink, light pink, black, very dark green, dark
  green, medium green, light green

Mono canvas, 4 meshes to the centimetre (10 meshes to the inch),
  (40.5 x 106.5 cm (16 x 42 in)

No 18 tapestry needle

Felt lining material; thread to match

Iron-on stiffener

Cardboard for inside bottom of bag

Two handles

Four brass feet (optional)

Masking tape, scissors, marker, ruler, needles

Stitch: Florentine over 4 meshes. Yarn doubled in needle
throughout.

This handsome bag (see page 48) is ideal for carrying
needlework projects. It is an extremely ambitious piece of work
and not recommended for the beginner.

Directions: Divide the 40.5 x 106.5-cm (16 x 42-in) canvas into
two pieces—one 40.5 x 71 cm (16 x 28 in) for the front, bottom
and back of the bag, the other 40.5 x 35.5 cm (16 x 14 in) for the
two side pieces. Tape all raw edges and mark the following
margins carefully:

On the larger piece mark an area 61 cm long by 30.5 cm (24 in
long by 12 in). The 61 cm (24 in) must now be divided into three
areas, two for the front and back of the bag measuring 25.5 x
30.5 cm (10 x 12 in) each, and one in between for the bottom,
measuring 10 x 30.5 cm (4 x 12 in). The front and back of the
bag will be 100 meshes high, while the centre piece for the
bottom measures 40 meshes. The mesh count must be accurate,
otherwise the lines of stitches in the three pieces will not match
up correctly.

Now divide the smaller piece of canvas into two strips for the
sides of the bag: each strip will be 10 x 25.5 cm (4 x 10 in),
separated by an unworked area of 5 cm (2 in). The mesh count
on each strip will be 100, corresponding to the height of the
front and the back of the bag, to which they will be sewn later.

The basic pattern of the bag is linear, a peaks and waves
design. Once you establish this initial line, the others follow in
exactly the same way. Start working on the canvas area which
corresponds to the front of the bag. Begin at the bottom centre
mesh with the light pink and complete one line working
upwards to either the left or right (see pattern diagram on page
49). After you have established this tracking line on both halves
of the canvas, fill in with the other colours until 100 meshes (or
25.5 cm or 10 in) are covered.

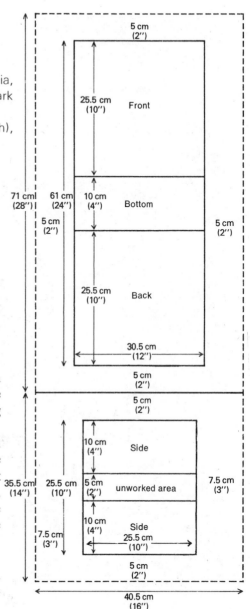

The unworked canvas divided into
working areas for the front, back,
sides and bottom of the bag.

The peaks and waves bag can be used for carrying knitting.

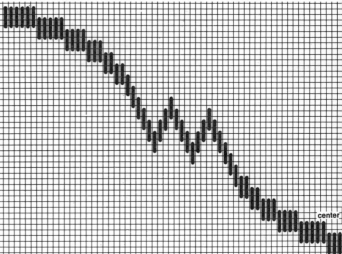

Do the same with the back. You should now have an area between the front and back, which will be the bottom of the bag, that is 10 cm (4 in) or 40 meshes long. Work this area according to the diagram on page 50. Notice that the pattern reverses itself in the middle.

Now take the smaller piece of canvas, 40.5 x 35.5 cm (16 x 14 in), which has been divided into two equal areas for the sides, and work the two side strips according to the diagram on the right. Make sure that you have an unworked area of canvas 5 cm (2 in) wide between the side strips.

Finishing: Separate the two side pieces by cutting along the centre of the unworked area of the canvas. Trim the canvas, leaving margins of about 2.5 cm (1 in) all around. Turn all raw edges under, making sure that you cut out a 4-mesh square at all corners to reduce the bulk when folding. Fold back the edges and sew them to the wrong side of the canvas. Cut a large piece of iron-on stiffener the size of the front, bottom, and back piece of canvas minus 0.6 cm (¼ in) on all sides. Cut two pieces for the side strips also, minus 0.6 cm (¼ in) on all sides. Place the finished needlework face down on an ironing board. Place the stiffener shiny or coated side down on the back of the canvas and press in place, following manufacturer's directions. (Be sure to read the exact instructions on the package for the use of iron-on stiffening, and follow them carefully.)

If desired, use four brass feet for the bottom of the bag. Insert each one through the right side of the work about 2 cm (¾ in) in from the sides and 1 cm (½ in) in from the front and back so that the prongs come through to the wrong side of the canvas. Hammer these prongs flat.

(Above left) Detail of front of bag. (Above) Half of the peaks and waves pattern for the front and back of the bag. Start at the centre and work upwards to left and right. This line is repeated exactly in all the colours.

Detail of side of the bag.

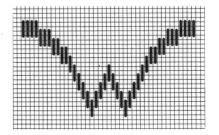

The pattern for the sides of the bag. Repeat this line.

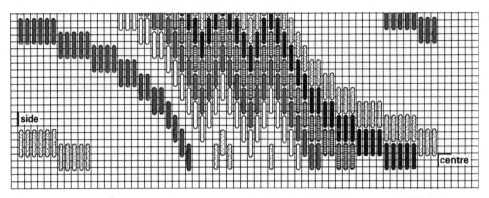

The peaks and waves pattern for the bottom of the bag. This chart corresponds to the upper left-hand quarter. To complete the bottom, reverse the chart and use the photo as a guide.

Now stitch the side panels to the front and back of the bag, one at a time, being very careful to match up the patterns. Sew them from the outside to make an invisible seam. Try to pick up at least every other thread on both pieces while you are sewing them together.

Cut a large piece of felt to the inner dimensions of the front, bottom, and back piece, allowing a 1.25-cm (½-in) seam area on each side. Cut two side panels to the inner dimensions of the sides plus 1.25 cm (½ in) also. Sew the side panels to the body of the lining. If you wish, you may cut a piece of felt for a pocket 18 x 20 cm (7 x 8 in). Hem one side and sew the pocket to the inside of the lining, hemmed side uppermost.

Cut a piece of stiff but pliable cardboard to the exact inner dimensions of the bag bottom. Slip it into the bottom of the bag. Place the felt lining, seams facing out, inside the bag. Slip-stitch the lining to the bag along the upper edges. Attach the handles securely to the inside between the lining and the canvas as you are sewing the lining in place.

Assembling and sewing the lining and handles of the bag.

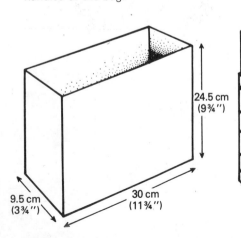

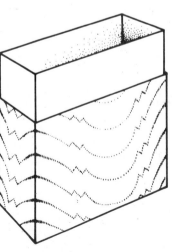

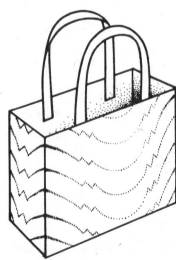

24.5 cm (9¾")

9.5 cm (3¾")

30 cm (11¾")

Candle flames table runner

Finished size: 25 x 61 cm (10 x 24 in)

Materials

Three-ply Persian yarn – gold 85 gr (3 oz), light olive 56 gr (2 oz),
    blue-grey 56 gr (2 oz), dark olive 28 gr (1 oz), red-orange 28 gr
    (1 oz)

Mono canvas, 4 meshes to the centimetre (10 meshes to the
    inch), 36 x 76 cm (14 x 30 in)

No 18 tapestry needle

Felt backing fabric; thread to match

Iron-on stiffener

Iron-on bonding fabric (optional)

Masking tape, scissors, marker, ruler, needles

Stitch: Florentine over 4 meshes. Yarn doubled in needle
throughout.

This pattern is one of overlapping diamonds with a row of single
diamonds in the centre. The pattern is worked in opposite
directions from the centre row out. The pattern gets its name
from the red stitches at the peak of each diamond, resembling
tiny flames (see the picture on page 53).

Directions: Cut a piece of canvas 36 x 76 cm (14 x 30 in) and bind
all sides with masking tape. Find the centre line of the canvas by
folding the piece in half horizontally. Draw a line across the
centre the width of the canvas. Measure this line and find its
middle point. Start the row of whole diamonds there. You
should have four and one half diamonds on each half. After
completing this row start the overlapping diamond pattern.
Remember that each side is worked opposite the other, out from
the centre. Continue until you reach the desired length. Yellow
is used to fill in the spaces between the completed diamonds at
each border edge.

Finishing: Block the needlework if necessary by ironing lightly on
the back with a warm iron and a damp cloth. Trim the excess
canvas to about 2.5 cm (1 in) from the finished work. Cut a small
square from each corner to avoid bulk while sewing. Turn the
edges to the wrong side and stitch down. Place the canvas face
down on an ironing board. Cut a piece of iron-on stiffener 1.25
cm (½ in) smaller than the finished work on all sides. Place it
shiny or coated side down on the wrong side of the canvas and
press in place, following manufacturer's directions. Cut a piece
of felt the same size as the completed table runner and
slip-stitch it neatly to the back.

If you wish, you may attach the felt backing with an iron-on
bonding material instead of sewing. Place strips of bonding
material on the back of the work, put the felt backing over it,
and press in place. Follow manufacturer's instructions.

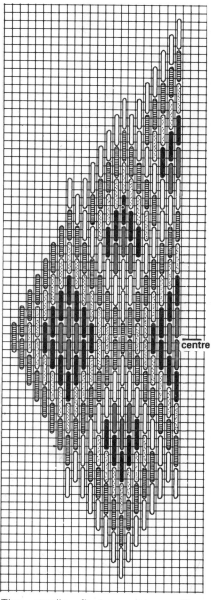

centre

The candle flames pattern. One
complete centre diamond and the
beginning of the overlapping diamond
pattern that surrounds it are shown.
Start from the centre of the canvas
and reverse the directions of the
overlapping diamonds as shown.

Candle flames napkin ring

Finished size: 6.4 x 15 cm (2½ x 6 in)

Materials

Three-ply Persian yarn – 2.75 metres (3 yards) each of light olive, blue-grey, dark olive, red-orange; 23 metres (25 yards) of gold

Mono canvas, 4 meshes to the centimetre (10 meshes to the inch), 10 x 20 cm (4 x 8 in)

No 18 tapestry needle

Grosgrain ribbon, 5 cm (2 in) wide x 16 cm (6½ in) long; thread to match

Iron-on stiffener

Masking tape, scissors, marker, ruler, needles

Stitches: Florentine over 4 meshes, whip stitch over edges. Yarn doubled in needle throughout.

Single flame tips on a gold background are used for this napkin ring. The edges are done in a whip stitch. Directions are given for one ring. Make as many as you like.

Directions: Cut a piece of canvas 10 x 20 cm (4 x 8 in). Tape all four sides. Measure an area 18 meshes wide by 70 meshes long and mark the margins. Find the centre and centre a single candle flame motif at that point, following the pattern diagram. There are seven motifs on the ring. When you have finished them, fill in the background with gold.

Finishing: Trim the canvas to 2 cm (¾ in) all around. Fold the raw edges of the long sides under, leaving 1 mesh above the finished line of stitching and 1 mesh on the fold at either side to be used for the whip stitch border. See that the holes of the canvas for this border line up one behind the other, front and back, to permit proper stitching. Finish this folded edge in the whip stitch using gold thread, being careful to push the needle through the double layer of mesh. Turn the two remaining side edges under and stitch to the back of the canvas. Cut a piece of iron-on stiffener slightly smaller than the finished ring and press it in place, following the directions given by the manufacturer. (Be sure to read the exact instructions on the package for the use of iron-on stiffening.)

With the right side of the work facing out, form a ring and slip-stitch the ends together with an invisible seam, sewing from the outside. Cut a piece of 5-cm (2-in) wide ribbon about 16 cm (6½ in) long and slip it inside the ring to measure the exact circumference. Remove the ribbon, and sew it together in a ring. Make sure that the seam of the ribbon is on the outside. Slip the ribbon ring inside the napkin ring and slip-stitch it in place.

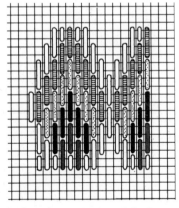

Pattern for a single candle flames motif.

Detail showing centre section of the candle flames table runner.

Candle flames napkin ring.

The candle flames table runner (see page 51) with four napkin rings.

Bargello tie in the Rickrack stitch pattern (instructions on page 56).

Diamond choker (instructions on page 58).

Shadow plaid spectacles case (instructions on page 57).

Old Florentine pincushion (instructions on page 55).

Old Florentine pincushion

Finished size: 11.5 x 15 cm (4½ x 6 in)

Materials

Three-ply Persian yarn – 9 metres (10 yards) each of lavender, violet,
    purple, rose, gold
Mono Canvas, 5 meshes to the centimetre (12 meshes to the inch),
    19 x 23 cm (7½ x 9 in)
No 18 tapestry needle
Felt backing; thread to match
Cotton wadding
Fine steel wool
Masking tape, scissors, marker, ruler, needles

Stitch: Over 4 meshes. Yarn doubled in needle throughout.

A pincushion is good for using up odds and ends of canvas and
yarn. Any convenient-size canvas will do.

Directions: Cut a piece of canvas to 19 x 23 cm (7½ x 9 in). Bind
all sides with masking tape. Find the centre of the canvas by
folding it in half vertically, and then horizontally. The centre is
where the folds meet. Mark it with a cross. Measure from the
centre out to find the margins of the finished work, 11.5 x 15 cm
(4½ x 6 in). Mark the margins lightly. Since this pattern consists
of three rows of three circles each, the centre of the canvas will
correspond to the centre of the middle circle. Start from the
centre, then, and work according to the pattern diagram.

Finishing: Trim the canvas to 1.25 cm (½ in) on all sides. Turn
the raw canvas under and stitch it to the back of the work. Cut a
piece of felt for backing the same size as the finished canvas.
Slip-stitch the felt backing to the edge of the needlework. Leave
a portion of one side open. Insert a filling of cotton wadding
with a layer of fine steel wool on top. (The steel wool will keep
needles clean and sharp.) Slip-stitch the opening closed.

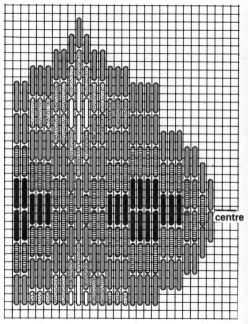

The old Florentine pattern. Begin at
the centre of the canvas.

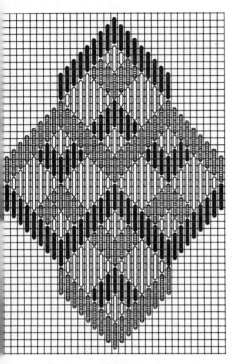

The rickrack pattern. Start work at the widest part of the tie.

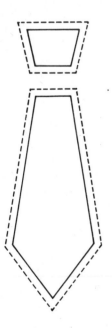

Tie outline showing the separate knot. Enlarge this diagram and trace it on to the canvas (or use a pre-knotted tie as your pattern).

Rickrack tie

Finished size: 10 x 45.5 cm (4 x 18 in)

Materials

Three-ply Persian yarn – slightly more than 14 gr (½ oz) each of red, blue, beige

Mono canvas, 5 meshes to the centimetre (12 meshes to the inch); two pieces 20 x 56 cm (8 x 22 in) and 15 x 17.5 cm (6 x 7 in)

No 20 tapestry needle

Lining material; thread to match

Elastic band or bow-tie clip

Masking tape, scissors, marker, ruler, needles

Stitches: Rickrack over 4 meshes, with a 1-mesh step up or down; diamond over 2 to 8 meshes; Hungarian stitch. Yarn single in needle throughout.

A needlework tie is an unusual and thoughtful gift for a man. Use a pre-knotted tie for your pattern; if it is unusually wide or long, be sure that the canvas is large enough to accommodate it. (The tie is pictured on page 54).

Directions: Cut two pieces of canvas, the longer one 20 x 56 cm (8 x 22 in) for the tie, the smaller one 15 x 17.5 cm (6 x 7 in) for the knot. Bind both pieces with masking tape. Draw an outline of a tie of desired length and width on the large piece of canvas, and an outline of a knot on the small one. Start working the pattern on the widest part of the tie, following the pattern diagram on the left. After the rickrack pattern is finished, fill in the large beige areas with the diamond stitch, and the smaller ones with the Hungarian stitch. When the body of the tie is done, work the knot, trying to match the pattern to the tie top so that the design has a continuous flowing effect.

Finishing: If necessary, block the tie and knot by ironing the work on the wrong side. Trim the canvas, leaving a 1.25-cm (½-in) margin all around the tie. Turn back the margins and sew them to the wrong side of the canvas. Cut a lining 1.25 cm (½ in) larger all around than the tie. Turn this 1.25-cm (½-in) allowance under, tack and press. Slip-stitch the lining to the back of the tie, wrong sides together, making sure to keep the edges of the tie and lining even.

Finish the knot in the same way. To give it a three-dimensional effect, stuff the knot with any soft material before sewing the lining completely in place. Pinch in the bottom corners of the knot when sewing it to the body of the tie. Use an elastic band or a bow-tie clip to fasten the tie in place.

Shadow plaid spectacles case

Finished size (folded): 16 x 8.2 cm (6¼ x 3¼ in)

Materials

Three-ply Persian yarn — less than 14 gr (½ oz) each of violet,
   fuchsia, dark green, light green
Mono canvas, 6 meshes to the centimetre (14 meshes to the inch),
   23 x 23 cm (9 x 9 in)
No 18 tapestry needle
Felt lining material; thread to match
Masking tape, scissors, marker, ruler, needles

Stitch: Over 5 meshes with a 1-mesh step up. Yarn single in needle
throughout.

Spectacles cases are a very attractive and practical way to use
up leftover canvas and yarns; they do not require much of
either. This project is pictured on page 54.

Directions: Cut the canvas to 23 x 23 cm (9 x 9 in) and tape it on
all sides. Measure the finished size, 16 x 16.5 cm (6¼ x 6½ in) —
the former being the length of the case, the latter the width
(before folding). Mark the outline on the canvas. This pattern is
worked vertically in stripes of two colours, a light green and
fuchsia stripe alternating with a dark green and violet stripe (see
pattern diagram). The pattern is eighteen stripes wide. Each
stripe consists of seventeen colour squares.
   Start the pattern at the bottom left-hand corner of the canvas
with the light green and work up the first stripe. Continue with
the next stripe and work up and then across until the entire
canvas is covered. Fill in any remaining top and bottom spaces
with the appropriate colours.

Finishing: Trim the canvas all around to a 1.25-cm (½-in)
margin. Bend this back and tack it to the wrong side of the
work. Cut a piece of felt the exact size of the finished needlework
before folding — 16 x 16.5 cm (6¼ x 6½ in). Felt makes a good
lining because it is soft and will not damage the glasses. Sew the
felt to the reverse side of the work. With the right side facing
out, carefully fold the needlework so that the two sides meet at
the centre back of the case. Carefully sew the case up this middle
point, matching the pattern so that the seam is invisible. Using
the same method, close the bottom of the case, matching the
pattern as you go. Remember to leave an opening at the top for
the insertion of the glasses.

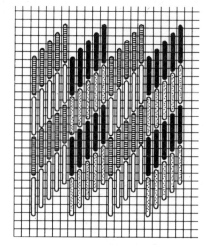

The shadow plaid pattern. Start at the
bottom left-hand corner of the canvas.

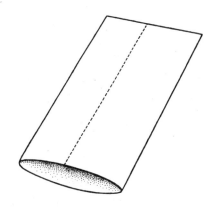

Fold the canvas so that the seam
runs down the centre back of the case.

Diamond choker

Finished size: 2 cm (13/16 in) wide, length as desired, plus ribbon tie

Materials

Pearl cotton No 3 – a few metres (yards) each of yellow, light green, dark green

Mono canvas, 7 meshes to the centimetre (18 meshes to the inch), 3.5 cm (1½ in) wide; length as desired

No 20 tapestry needle

Ribbon, 2 cm (¾ in) wide, length as desired; thread to match

Scissors, tape measure, ruler, marker, needles

Stitches: Gobelin over 3 meshes, Florentine over 2 meshes. Yarn single in needle throughout.

A choker can be done in a few hours and makes an attractive accessory. (See the photograph on page 54.) The same method can be used to make a headband as well.

Directions: Cut a strip of mono canvas just over 3.5 cm (about 1½ in) wide and the length of your neck or head measurement plus 5 cm (2 in) for margins. Count off 15 meshes for the width and draw two margins the entire length of the strip. Fold the canvas back along these lines and tack the edges down lightly with a tacking stitch. You should now have a strip of canvas 15 meshes wide by the desired length. Fold the strip in half to find the centre front. Start at the centre and work according to the diagram, with the centre front corresponding to the centre of the middle diamond of the choker. Work the three diamonds first. Then complete the remainder with the Gobelin stitch over 3 meshes to form the stripes. Sew through the double thickness of canvas, pulling out the tacking threads as you come to them. Sew right over the edges of the canvas at the last stitch on each row in order to give a finished edge to the work.

Finishing: Bend back the unworked ends of the raw canvas and sew them to the wrong side of the choker. Centre a long ribbon 2 cm (¾ in) wide and slip-stitch it to the back of the choker, leaving a long end on each side for tying.

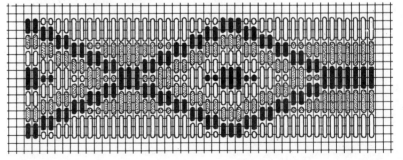

The diamond choker pattern. Start at the centre of the canvas and work to each end.

A handsome Bargello rug, done on No 5 rug canvas with heavy rug wool.

Pineapple picture

Finished size (unframed): 23 x 28.5 cm (9 x 11¼ in)

Materials

Three-ply Persian yarn – 28 gr (1 oz) each of yellow, red, dark brown,
  light green, light olive, cream; a few metres (yards) of dark olive
Mono canvas, 6 meshes to the centimetre (14 meshes to the inch),
  33 x 39 cm (13 x 15¼ in)
No 18 tapestry needle
Masking tape, scissors, ruler, marker

Stitches: Over 2 meshes for the pineapple, brick stitch for the leaves,
Hungarian stitch for the background, split stitch for outlining the
leaves and pineapple. Yarn single in needle throughout.

This picture was adapted from an original wash drawing. A
photostat was made of the picture and then blown up to the size
of the finished work. The photostat was traced onto the canvas
and the stitches were then worked out.

Directions: Cut the canvas to 33 x 39 cm (13 x 15¼ in) and tape
all four sides. If desired, lightly trace an outline of the pineapple
and the leaves onto the canvas to serve as a guide while working.
  Follow the diagrams on page 61 for the stitches and the photo
below for the colours. Notice that all stitches are over 2 meshes
of the canvas, except for the Hungarian stitch background. The

(Below) The original wash drawing of
the pineapple and the photostat made
from it. (Right) The Pineapple Picture
translated into Bargello.

Outline pattern for the pineapple. Enlarge it and draw it on canvas as a guide to stitching.

The split stitch.

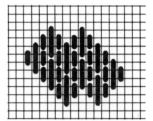

The Hungarian stitch pattern used for the background.

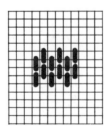

The brick stitch pattern used for the leaves.

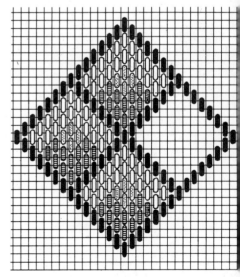

The pineapple pattern.

split stitch, a crewel stitch, was used to outline the leaves in dark olive and to outline the pineapple in dark brown.

To make the split stitch, make a straight stitch. Draw it flat. Come up into the centre of the stitch you have just made, splitting the yarn (see diagram). Continue this way, making a smooth row of flat stitches.

Finishing: When the background has been finished, turn the work over and trim any long or hanging threads on the back. If the picture is out of shape, iron it lightly on the wrong side with a damp cloth. It is best to have this picture professionally framed, in any way you wish.

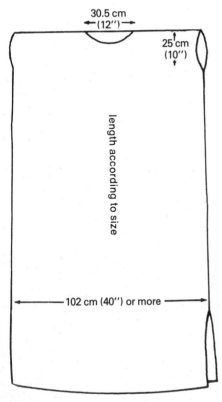

30.5 cm
←(12″)→

25 cm
(10″)

length according to size

← 102 cm (40″) or more →

Make the caftan according to this simple pattern.

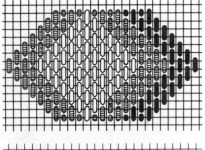

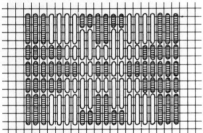

Patterns for the caftan trim. See photo on facing page for colour and pattern sequence.

Moroccan caftan

Materials

Caftan (see instructions below)

Mono canvas, 6 meshes to the centimetre (14 meshes to the inch); width and length as desired

Three-ply Persian yarn – assorted colours, a few metres of each

No 18 tapestry needle

Thread to match caftan

Scissors, marker, needles

Stitches: Over various meshes of the canvas. Yarn single in needle throughout.

Caftans have become extremely popular for lounge and evening wear. Here is a way to use Bargello embroidery to trim a caftan. The patterns are based on authentic Moroccan embroideries.

Directions: Make up a caftan according to your own pattern, or follow the instructions given below. Choose a neutral, lightweight fabric that is easily washed or cleaned. Use bright contrasting colours for the Bargello trim. Make sure that the wool used for the embroidery is colourfast and dry-cleanable.

Cut strips of the canvas about 5 cm (2 in) wide by 2.5 cm (1 in) more than the desired length of the trim. Count off the number of meshes for the width desired and fold back the excess on either side. Tack the margins to the back of the strip with a tacking stitch that can be pulled out as you work. Make sure that the meshes at the front of the fold line up with the meshes at the back to permit proper stitching. Sew through both layers of canvas when working. Sew right over the folded edges with each last stitch to give a neat finished side. Follow the diagrams for the patterns for each strip. Repeat the patterns but vary the colours from strip to strip. Make as many as you wish, depending on the size of the caftan and how much trimming you want.

Finishing: Bend back the unfinished ends of each strip and sew them securely to the back of the piece. Arrange each strip on the front of the caftan and slip-stitch in place.

Caftan

Materials

3.5 to 4.5 metres (4 or 5 yards) of lightweight fabric, 102 cm (40 in) or more wide

Thread to match

Decorative fastenings or hooks and eyes for shoulders

Needles, pins, scissors

Directions: Choose a neutral, lightweight fabric 102 cm (40 in) or more wide, that is easily washed or cleaned. Measure the length from your shoulders to the floor. Add 15 cm (6 in) and double this figure. This is the length of the fabric you will need to make the caftan. Fold the fabric in half lengthwise and cut it in two pieces. With the wrong sides together, sew a 2-cm (¾-in) shoulder seam on each side of the top edge, allowing a 30.5-cm (12-in) neck opening. (You may allow a larger opening for the neck and use decorative fasteners or hooks and eyes to adjust the fit.) Beginning 25 cm (10 in) down from the shoulder seams, stitch the front and back of the caftan together for the side seams. Hem the neck and arm openings. Measure the length and hem the bottom. If you wish to have a side slit, do not sew the side seams down to the floor. Add the Bargello trim to the front.

(Left) The Moroccan caftan. (Above) Detail of the Bargello trim placed vertically on the front of the caftan.

A Bargello wall hanging in the form of a kite.

Bibliography

Barnes, Charles, and Blake, David P., *Bargello and Related Stitchery*, Hearthside Press, Inc, Great Neck, NY, 1971.

Christensen, Jo Ippolito, and Ashner, Sonie Shapiro, *Bargello Stitchery*, Sterling Publishing Co, Inc, New York, NY, 1972.

Scobey, Joan, and McGrath, Lee Parr, *Do-It-All-Yourself Needlepoint*, Essandess Special Editions, Division of Simon and Schuster, Inc, New York, NY, 1971.

Silverstein, Mira, *Fun With Bargello*, Charles Scribner's Sons, New York, NY, 1971.

Snook, Barbara, *Florentine Embroidery*, Charles Scribner's Sons, New York, NY, 1967.

Editors of Sunset Books and Sunset Magazine, *Needlepoint: Techniques and Projects*, Lane Books, Menlo Park, California, 1972.

Williams, Elsa S., *Bargello, Florentine Canvas Work*, Van Nostrand, Reinhold Co, New York, NY, 1967.

Suppliers

All the materials mentioned in this book are readily available at needlework shops and in the needlework sections of most department stores. The following is a partial list of suppliers from whom you can order by mail.

E. J. Arnold & Son Ltd,
Butterley Street,
Leeds,
LS10 1AX

The Campden Needlecraft Centre,
High Street,
Chipping Campden,
Gloucestershire

Dryad,
Northgates,
Leicester,
LE1 4QR

The Needlewoman Shop,
146/8 Regent Street,
London,
W1R 6BA

J. Hyslop Bathgate & Co,
Victoria Works,
Galashiels,
Scotland